Co-Surviving Cancer

The Guide for Caregivers, Family Members and Friends of Adults Living with Cancer

Katie Brown. OPN-CG

Cancer Survivor, Co-Survivor, and Oncology Patient Navigator

Dear Co Survivor,

If you are someone who feels deeply that you are surviving the traumatic experience of cancer alongside someone you care about, this book is for you! I use the term Co-survivor because of the shared emotional experiences of cancer between patients and the people who care for them. Co-survivors can be family members, friends, and healthcare providers.

At the age of 22 I became a cancer survivor. My cancer was found in its earliest stages. While I have had long term emotional and physical side effects, to date that cancer has not returned. I am lucky.

At the age of 29 my father was diagnosed with a late stage cancer. There were few treatment options for him and the treatments he did have were brutal. He lived 11 months and 21 days after his diagnosis. He was not as lucky.

Each cancer experience is different and every caregiving experience is just as different, but there are many common feelings, emotions and practical hurdles that we all face.

When my dad was diagnosed, suddenly and without hesitation I became his caregiver. I delved head first into the medical community, cancer care, patient navigation and advocacy. There was no training or guidance. There was little support. Pretty much everything we experienced was trial by fire. I was frustrated and isolated and so very tired.

Somehow, we make it through difficult times because that's just the way life works. But what if caregiving for someone with cancer came with directions, some support and a lot less trauma?

Over the last decade I've benefited from a lot of resources, collaboration within the cancer community and professional training. If you're reading this book, you don't have a decade to learn all the things I have. You weren't given a handbook or an outline or any training on how to deal with the cancer diagnosis of a loved one. You need help and you need it now.

Maybe you don't know where to start first? This book will be your guide to understanding your role, your relationship with your loved one, getting organized and making the most of this experience.

As difficult and as hard as caregiving can be, it is also an honor. Caregivers are unsung heroes. Once you have the tools to caregiving, you will become a Co-Survivor and can make the most of your experience in this important role.

Over the years I've supported and cared for thousands of patients and their families first through my foundation, The Lung Cancer Support Community, and now through my work as Vice President of Support and Survivorship with the LUNGevity Foundation. I support patients and families by providing emotional support, survivorship conferences, education and patient navigation.

I would like to share what I've learned with you. This book will serve as a guide for caregivers, family members and friends of someone with cancer.

Best Hopes, Katie Brown

This book is dedicated to Rickey Brown, whose love and support enabled me to be the best caregiver I could be and for Hunter and Kennedy, our biggest blessings.

DEFINING YOUR ROLE

- Different Types of Caregivers
- Defining Your Caregiving Role

I.   IN THE BEGINNING

- Getting Your Medical Degree? (not really- but almost)
- Learning About Your Loved One's Diagnosis
- The Medical Team / Meeting the Medical Team
- Don't be Afraid of Second Opinions
- What are Clinical Trials
- Financial Issues
- Palliative Care- What it is and What It's Not
- Additional Support for the Patient

II.   BECOMING AN ADVOCATE

- Doctor's Visits
- Talking to Your Employer
- Long Distance Caregiving
- Creating your Caregiver Action Plan (CAP)
- Asking for and Receiving Help

III.   CAREGIVER FATIGUE

- Depression
- Caregiver Burnout

IV.   RESOURCES FOR CAREGIVERS

- Organizations That Support Caregivers
- Psychosocial Help
- Grief and Bereavement

V.   LIFE AFTER CAREGIVING

DIFFERENT TYPES OF CAREGIVERS

What are caregivers?

Becoming a caregiver is a job that no one applied for. There isn't a manual or a medical care team that cares for the caregiver. You do dozens of things at once in the daily caregiving of your loved one and in the daily responsibilities of your lives- usually without applause or fanfare. Caregivers are often unsung heroes in the cancer journey who rarely ask for help. I want to change that.

Sometimes a decision is made on who will be the patient's caregiver. Most times it's a given who the patients caregiver will be; no one had to ask.

Most people have a preconceived notion of caregivers. The most common idea of a caregiver is your doctor or nurse or professionals who care for the elderly. Before cancer barreled into your life did you pay much attention to what caregiving is? Or who would make a good caregiver?

What does a cancer caregiver do? Here are some of the things that a cancer caregiver does:

- Cancer care
- Provide emotional support
- Transportation to and from medical visits/treatment
- Consult with patient on treatment decisions
- Managing side effects
- Make and/or prepare meals
- Help keep track of/administer medications
- Help the patient with person hygiene
- Housekeeping and lawn maintenance
- Facilitating communication around the cancer care of the patient
- Financial responsibilities
- Legal Issues

- Scheduling medical appointments
- *On top of all the other responsibilities they had *before* cancer entered their lives

All of this new responsibility can be very overwhelming, but it doesn't have to be the sole responsibility of one person.

There are different types of cancer caregivers.

Caregivers can be paid professionals, spouses, family members, or close friends.

Family Caregivers

A family caregiver is someone who is not paid or trained to assist a cancer patient. Their role is pivotal to daily life and helps the cancer patient survive with a reasonable quality of life.

There can be primary and secondary family caregivers.

Primary caregivers are usually (but not exclusively) those who live with the patient. Spouses or parents of the patient or adult children of the patient are examples of family caregivers who live with the patient.

Secondary caregivers can be additional family members like siblings or additional adult children or relatives of the patient.

Most family caregivers describe their reaction to learning their loved one has cancer in violent terms: a punch in the stomach, hitting a deep pothole, a lightning strike, being frozen or speechless, being hit by a truck or having the rug pulled out from under them. Becoming a caregiver was sudden and most times it came without warning.

Some family caregivers become caregivers by default because they are a spouse or relative of the patient. There was never any question that they would be caring for their loved one. But now what, they ask?

Other times becoming a caregiver happened by default because a person is related to the patient and the patient lives alone.

Sometimes it happens by accident as you find yourself stepping up where no one else will. You suddenly take on more responsibilities and assist in the patient's daily life and medical care.

What inspires family caregivers? Love, a sense of loyalty or moral duty, even guilt.

Most caregivers I have spoken to feel honored to care for someone they love. Those people also report sometimes feeling very overwhelmed. Their love for the patient and desire to help them get "better" sometimes is what prevents them from asking for help. They want to shoulder the responsibility alone.

However your story began, you are now a caregiver working to become a Co-Survivor.

Professional Caregivers

A professional caregiver is your medical team and independent persons hired and paid to perform care to patients in need. These are people who have been professionally trained to administer care and support to patients. They can be patient navigators, advocates, physical therapists, social workers, home health aides and other professionals who deliver physical and emotional care.

Patient navigators or advocates provided by the patients treating hospital can find local and financial resources for the patient. These caregivers can handle some of the practical issues a cancer patient faces.

Aside from the medical team treating the disease, not everyone will have access to or experience the different types of professional caregivers. Some hospitals provide patient navigators, social workers and other survivorship resources for patients.

Long Distance Caregivers

When a person does not live with the patient, but provides emotional or practical support, they are what I call a "long-distance" caregiver. This person may provide emotional support by phone or email, do online research or be the person who keeps everyone up to date on the condition of the patient. While this person isn't involved in daily care, their role is important too. They can offer additional support and resources and encourage the patient and their primary and secondary caregivers and family during the cancer experience. Friends and distant relatives can be long distance caregivers.

Some families rally around the patient to help with care. Those people are called family caregivers.

DEFINING YOUR CAREGIVING ROLE

Communication is important after someone you care about is diagnosed with cancer. Cancer affects the entire family and it touches friends, neighbors and coworkers too. Things will change. You have to work together to find your "new normal" during cancer care.

Cancer is an equal opportunity threat to your quality of life and survivorship, but there is good news for many people. It's not always a death sentence. There ARE survivors and there IS hope. Better treatments, medications, medical professionals and caregivers make surviving cancer possible.

Because of the uncertainty of cancer, emotions can run high. There are practical issues like medical treatment, time off work, disability, financial cost, and transportation logistics on top of your "normal" everyday life responsibilities. There is a long list of other issues that arise during cancer care. After a cancer diagnosis your lives change and so might your relationships.

Communicate with your loved one what it means to you to be a caregiver. Set expectations and walk thru scenarios. Make a list of the people in your lives that you want to share this experience with and which one of them may be of help to you during this time. Make a list of responsibilities and map out a plan.

What is your role? Are you the primary caregiver? Are you the secondary caregiver? Are you the person who schedules care and keeps everyone in the family updated? Are you a long-distance caregiver? For long distance caregivers- what are the rules of this role and what are the patients' boundaries? Keep in mind that roles, rules and boundaries may change with each stage of cancer treatment and care. The patient navigates his/her experience.

Talk to the patient. If your loved one is someone who doesn't like to discuss emotional or sensitive issues or if you are someone uncomfortable with discussing those issues, start off pragmatically.

"John (patient) this is what needs to be done right now. I am able to do (X,Y,Z), what would you like me to do? Is there anything you don't want me to do? Let's make a list together and figure out the logistics."

I've known some patients who don't actively participate in their cancer care at all and are more comfortable leaving every aspect of their treatments and home care to their primary caregiver while they concentrate on getting through treatment.

Other patients worked to build themselves a care community of family and close friends to help them through the hardest parts of their cancer treatments.

Here's how my role as a somewhat unconventional primary caregiver surfaced.

The diagnosis:

My dad's diagnosis came out of the blue. He was 63 and had a job that required yearly physicals. My entire life my dad was rarely ever sick. But late in the summer of 2002 he had a chronic ache in his lower back and then one day he lost his voice. He experienced no illness or pain to explain the loss of his voice. Those symptoms made his family doctor take notice and send him to an ear, nose and throat specialist. A few additional doctors and some scans later revealed two masses in his left lung.

When he told me about his doctor's appointment and the test results, I could tell he was being vague and careful with his words. Even at the age of 29, I was still his little girl. "Well Katherine," *He only called me Katherine when I was in trouble!* "They found "something" on my lung. Not sure exactly what it is but the doctor's will figure it out."

I went home that night and did an internet search on "lung mass, lung tumor, lung cancer" and was horrified at everything I read. I took a lot of notes and printed off a lot of pages to stick in my "dad" folder.

My parents asked me to join them at the appointment with the Pulmonologist. I asked my dad if it was ok if I asked the doctor some questions and he said yes. I pulled out a page long list of questions and proceeded to intelligently ask the pulmonologist all the questions on my list. My parents just stared at me. They had no clue that I had researched the possibilities and knew what to ask the doctor.

While my dad had someone who lived in the home to take care of him physically if needed, my mother was a limited English speaker. She was not someone who could help at doctor's appointments, ask questions, keep notes, and help him take medications. She could not make payments or manage financial responsibilities. Because I lived nearby and proved capable, all those things fell to me when he was eventually diagnosed with extensive stage lung cancer.

Because I had taken the initiative to learn more about his disease and ask questions- all the logistical responsibilities of a caregiver fell to me. No one asked me if I would be willing to do it. It just happened and I was honored to do it.

I tried to openly communicate everything with my dad, but he only wanted to talk logistics. He didn't want to discuss anything emotional or the fact that his prognosis was not a good one. He wanted me to handle all the medical and financial responsibilities and he would concentrate on getting through the treatments and eating and drinking the right things. He wanted us to watch TV together and spend time doing family things- not talk about cancer.

Over the years I've learned a great deal about caregiving from supporting patients and talking to other caregivers. It's important to follow the cues of the patient. It's important to find out what their boundaries are and what they can and cannot handle. Even though they have cancer, they are still the person they were before cancer. Meaning, if your loved one is introverted or communicates very little- don't expect that to change overnight or even at all. If your loved one was needy before cancer, chances are they may be even more so after cancer. If your loved one was someone who did things independently before cancer, it may be difficult for them to ask for help even after a cancer diagnosis.

My dad was strong and stoic. He was not an extrovert and did not have needless conversations. He never asked anyone for help- *ever*. Looking back, my dad could not handle having those types of conversations with me. He did not want to talk about death or dying. He did not want to hear or talk about prognosis. He trusted his doctor. He never considered a second opinion. He didn't want to ask any questions. He did not want to hear or talk about anything negative. He never complained about feeling bad or side effects.

So we (my mother and I) shouldered all of that. While I'm sure he thought he was protecting us, we were protecting him. And he frustrated the hell out of us more than once! But I'll get to that.

It was a given that I would be at every doctor's appointment and every chemotherapy treatment. The pharmacy techs all knew my face when I came to pick up his medications. Everything I had been doing in my life – being a wife and a mom to a 4-year-old, my last year of school and working full time all had to juggle around being a caregiver for my dad. It was the most difficult period in our lives.

In hindsight there were so many things that could have made things easier for us. One of them would have been to have a frank discussion about what my role would be and what I was able to do.

CONVERSATION POINT:
Here are some suggestions to help you kick start that conversation.

- Will you let me participate in doctors' appointments and your cancer care?
- Who else are you comfortable going to your doctor's appointments with?
- Who will be taking you to your treatments?
- Who will you call when you don't feel well or are experiencing side effects?

- Is there someone that can help with yard work, housekeeping, meals, etc...?
- In the event you are unable to make decisions, who will you name as your healthcare proxy?

It takes time to work out how you will navigate through a loved one's cancer care. Ask your loved one to work with you to make a list of things that need to be done and a list of people who might be able to help. Sometimes that is a long list of names. Other times that list has only one name- yours.

One common challenge is caregiving for a family member who is very private. This person doesn't want to share with you the full scope of their medical history or diagnosis. They don't want people in their homes and may not want help with financial issues. This person will be a challenge to help and it may be harder to define the parameters of your caregiving role.

My dad was one of these very private people. We never talked about financial or legal issues until there was a roadblock or problem in his paperwork or care. Knowing his insurance plan and having an account of his finances and bills would have helped greatly. I felt like I was constantly chasing down information. Knowing what I know today, I would have done things very differently.

One suggestion I have is creating The List. For some reason people rarely argue with lists! They are black and white and in print and can be filled out separately or together, helping those who may have communication issues in their relationship.

I helped an adult daughter who was caring for her mom create The List to try to solve the frustrating fact that her mother, while battling an extensive stage cancer, continued to treat her as if she were a child rather than a partner in her cancer journey. Her mother shielded her from scan results and the severity of her disease. She didn't share with her daughter the stage of her cancer, treatment options or the number of co-pays she would have to pay. The List helped to define boundaries and roles. Patient-mom could fill some of it out while alone and then caregiver-daughter was able to ask questions to clarify her mom's needs and wishes when they were together.

Today, The List- something similar to what I had created- is known as a Caregiver Action Plan (CAP) and you can read more about it in Section II.

IN THE

BEGINNING

GETTING YOUR MEDICAL DEGREE - *Not really but it sure feels like it.*

Learning about cancer terms, treatments and the healthcare system can make you feel like you are in medical school. There are few resources out there that put terms into easy to read (and understand) definitions. Where can you find information about your loved one's cancer?

The internet:

While the internet can be a scary place for information, there are hundreds of websites, articles and videos about cancer that you can access from the comfort of your personal computer. How do you know which ones are trustworthy and accurate?

Credible websites are websites that display information that has been vetted for accuracy. WebMD, The National Cancer Institute, The National Institutes of Health, The US Department of Health and Human Services and The American Cancer Society are just a few examples of credible websites. You can also visit the website of the hospital your loved one is being treated at and browse the resources they have listed on their website. Oftentimes there will be a listing of cancer websites and one may be specific to the type of cancer your loved one has.

For example, if someone impacted by lung cancer goes to their hospital website, they may see LUNGevity Foundation listed as a resource. The information found on the LUNGevity Foundation website has been vetted by a world-renowned science board. There are many areas within the website that educate you about the disease and commonly used terms. There are videos and printouts. There are sections of the website that provide information about the different types of treatments specifically for lung cancer and there are listings of resources for patients and caregivers seeking help with practical or emotional issues.

Depending on the type of cancer your loved one has, this is the type of website you need to find to be your source of online education.

List some credible websites here that you can refer to:

Books & Brochures:

When your loved one was diagnosed, he or she was probably given a patient folder or bag of booklets that tell a little more about the disease. That is a good place to begin. Read those booklets and handouts. Look at the bottom or back of those handouts and brochures to see if there are websites listed on them that may provide even more information. Because these materials were given to the patient, chances are they have been vetted by the facility or doctor and can be trusted.

Create a folder or binder of your own with page prints and notes about your loved one's cancer and information about the types of treatment for that cancer. [Keep a list of credible websites that you find helpful and notes on where to find resources that you may not need until a later date.]

Visit your loved one's treatment center. Most hospitals have a patient resource center with books and brochures that have been pre-approved and deemed credible. Check out everything that may apply to your loved one's cancer and your personal situation.

What are some books or brochures you've found helpful? List them below so that you can refer back to them or refer them to other caregivers and healthcare providers:

_____

_____

_____

_____

_____

_____

_____

LEARNING ABOUT YOUR LOVED ONE'S DIAGNOSIS

If you are a primary caregiver and/or advocate for someone with cancer, you need to know their diagnosis. This may sound like a no brainer but sometimes even patients don't know what their medical diagnosis is. It's not that their doctor didn't tell them. Chances are they simply didn't hear anything after the word "cancer". The world as they knew it seemed to sway and flip and digesting such foreign news could have been emotionally difficult.

In 1995 I was given my cancer diagnosis over the phone, during the day, while I was working as a customer service representative for IBM. That was not the kind of call I was used to taking! While my cancer was found very early, the shock of the word "cancer" and the subsequent worst-case scenarios the nurse was going over on the phone with me made me think the absolute worst was going to happen to me. I just knew I was dying. I was dying right then and there in an IBM cubical. Obviously, I was not-but that shows you how our emotions can impact the information that we process.

I've had a patient tell me he had non-smokers lung cancer. There is no such diagnosis as people who smoke, and those without a smoking history, can have the same type of lung cancer. What he meant to say was that he is a lifeline never-smoker who was diagnosed with lung cancer.

Let's delve a little deeper. What sub-type and/or stage of cancer is it? Does he have any genetic mutations? Are there any metastasis (spread) to other sites? What stage is his cancer? What are the standard types of treatments for this type of cancer? These are all things you should know about your loved one's diagnosis.

CONVERSATION POINT:

Here are some suggested questions you can ask your loved one's doctor regarding their diagnosis. Remember to ask the patient if it is ok for you to ask these questions to the doctor.

Remember that the patient may not want to be present or they may not want to know the answer to certain questions:

- What type of cancer is it?

  _____

- Is there a subtype of this cancer?

  _____

  What tests did you do to determine the type of cancer?

  _____

- Is it hereditary? Are family members at risk?

  _____

- Is this cancer genetic? Are there genetic tests for this cancer type?

  _____

- Has this cancer metastasized (spread)? And if yes, to which parts of the body?

  _____

- What stage is this cancer? What does that mean? Prognosis?

  _____

- What are the treatment recommendation for this type and stage of cancer?

  _____

- Are there a lot of treatment options for this type and stage of cancer?

  _____

- Are there targeted therapies and/or clinical trials for this type of cancer?

  _____

- What are the side effects of the treatment you are recommending?

  _____

- Are you a specialist in this type of cancer?

  _____

- Should I seek a second opinion and can you help me with that?

  _____

- Where can we find more information about this cancer?

  _____

- Where can we find support for people diagnosed with this cancer type?

  _____

THE MEDICAL TEAM

Many facilities are now promoting that they are providing precision medicine and practicing patient centered care. This is a polished way of saying that patients are at the forefront of what they do and treatments are being tailored to everyone. That sounds great to me, but in retrospect, it's terrifying to think that patients weren't at the top of mind before. With a renewed emphasis on patient centered care, there may be new specialties and resources available to patients now than there were just 5 years ago. That's incredibly encouraging.

Knowing what these medical experts and specialists do will help you as you advocate for your loved one. There may be many members of the cancer care team.

Let's define some of the common specialists in cancer care and what they do:

Medical Oncologist- He/she is probably the doctor you will see most often. This doctor treats patients with chemotherapy and other cancer fighting drugs. This doctor usually oversees the patient's general cancer care with checkup tests and follow-up tests. There are many different types of chemotherapies and cancer fighting drugs.

Radiation Oncologist- He/she targets cancer with radiation therapy and works with the medical oncologist to shrink tumors or eliminate tumors. Radiation can be given as a curative modality, either alone or in combination with surgery and/or chemotherapy. It may also be used palliatively, to relieve symptoms in patients with incurable cancers. A radiation oncologist may also use radiation to treat some benign diseases and benign tumors. Radiation oncologists work closely with other specialists as part of the multi-disciplinary cancer team.

Surgical Oncologist- He/she removes cancer with surgery. Usually a surgical oncologist will be specialized in one or more types of cancer.

Radiologist- A doctor who uses a variety of imaging techniques such as X-ray radiography, ultrasound, computed tomography (CT), nuclear medicine including positron emission tomography (PET), and magnetic resonance imaging (MRI) to diagnose and/or treat diseases.

Hematologists- Physicians whose routine work mainly includes the care and treatment of patients with hematological diseases, although some may also work at the hematology laboratory viewing blood films and bone marrow slides under the microscope, interpreting various hematological test results and blood clotting test results. In some institutions, hematologists also manage the hematology laboratory.

Gynecologic Oncologist- focuses on cancers of the female reproductive system, including ovarian cancer, uterine cancer, vaginal cancer, cervical cancer, and vulvar cancer. As specialists, they have extensive training in the diagnosis and treatment of these cancers.

Clinical Nurse- this is a nurse that may assist patients in the infusion room and during procedures.

Nurse Practitioners- (NPs) manage acute and chronic medical conditions, both physical and mental, through history and physical exam and the ordering of diagnostic tests and medical treatments. NPs are qualified to diagnose medical problems, order treatments, perform advanced procedures, prescribe medications, and make referrals for a wide range of acute and chronic medical conditions within their scope of practice. In addition to building upon and expanding their nursing knowledge and skills, the nurse practitioner also learns medicine and uses medical diagnoses and medical treatments in their practice. NPs work in hospitals, private offices, clinics, and nursing homes/long term care facilities.

Patient Navigator- people who take individual patients through the continuum of healthcare as it pertains to their specific disease, ensuring that any and all barriers to that care are resolved and that each stage of care is as quick and seamless as possible.

Oncology Social Worker- Social workers specially trained in cancer care and dedicated to helping patients and families navigate the health care system, and manage the many challenges of living with cancer.

Clinical Oncology Dietician/Nutritionist- Their work is wide-ranging, from helping a patient deal with lifestyle changes and side effects to providing nutritional recipes to help keep up a patient's strength during treatment. An oncology nutritionist is a registered dietitian who is a certified specialist in oncology (CSO), a credential received through the American Dietetic Association.

Physician's Assistant- (or PA) is a nationally certified and state-licensed medical professional. PAs practice medicine on healthcare teams with physicians and other providers. They practice and prescribe medication in all 50 states, the District of Columbia, the majority of the U.S. territories and the uniformed services.

Pharmacists- are healthcare professionals who practice in pharmacy, the field of health sciences focusing on safe and effective medication use. A pharmacist is a member of the health care team directly involved with patient care

Palliative Care –is a multidisciplinary approach to specialized medical care for people with serious illnesses. It focuses on providing patients with relief from the symptoms, pain, physical stress, and mental stress of a serious illness—whatever the diagnosis. The goal of such therapy is to improve quality of life for both the patient and the family. Palliative care is provided by a team of physicians, nurses, and other health professionals who work together with the primary care physician and referred specialists (or, for patients who don't have those, hospital or hospice staff) to provide an extra layer of support. It is appropriate at any age and at any stage in a serious illness and can be provided along with curative treatment.

Sources:
Physician's Assistant www.aapa.org
Wikipedia www.en.wikipedia.org
Harold P. Freeman Patient Navigation Institute www.hpfreemanpni.org

OUR MEDICAL TEAM CONSISTS OF:

GP

_____

ONCOLOGIST

_____

SURGEON

_____

NURSE(S)

_____

SOCIAL WORKER

_____

RADIATION

_____

SURGEON

_____

SPECIALIST

_____

SPECIALIST

_____

SPECIALIST

_____

OTHER/NOTES_____

_____

_____

_____

_____

_____

_____

_____

_____

_____

_____

_____

_____

_____

_____

MEETING THE MEDICAL TEAM

Now that you know some of the names of some of the 'players' of this team of healthcare providers, you, along with the patient, must decide in what ways you interact with them.

You may not be going to doctor's appointment or privy to medical conversations, but knowing who is on the medical team and understanding what they do will help in your conversations with your loved one.

If you are a caregiver that will not be accompanying the patient to medical appointments, you can skip to the next chapter. If you're not entirely sure, keep reading.

If you are a caregiver who will be accompanying the patient to every appointment, every infusion, every test and every meeting than you will be sharing in the real-time experience of treatment care.

CONVERSATION POINT:

WITH PATIENT

- Talk to your loved one about your role within their treatment care.
- Is the patient comfortable with you going to doctors' appointments?
- Is he/she comfortable with you asking questions and getting answers about their condition?
- How much does the patient want you to advocate on their behalf?
- Does the patient want or mind you researching different treatments or options and asking about those on your behalf?
- Ask the patient what their boundaries are. What do they expect of you and what are your expectations?
- Make a plan to talk to the doctor and medical team together.

There are a lot of advantages to sharing in the experience of treatment care.

You will be able to listen and learn what the healthcare provider is recommending to the patient.

You may be able to contribute to the conversation and ask clarifying questions.

You may be able to be the patients advocate and speak up about side effects, questions and any concerns. You may be able to ask about things you researched and read about.

Once the patient has decided how involved their caregiver will be in their treatment care, it's time to talk to the medical team.

You may be a vital part of the decision-making process.

Talk to the patient about their expectations and what your personal goals are before treatment begins when possible.

If you are someone who became a caregiver after treatment began, the medical team can get you up to speed on the treatment and status of the patient.

CONVERSATION POINT:

WITH MEDICAL TEAM

- Ask for a meeting with the patient's oncologist, nurse navigator or case manager
- Inform the medical team about the different ways the caregiver will be involved in the patient's cancer care, in decision making, and how much access the caregiver should have to medical information and sign any necessary paperwork required to give you that authorization.

Some Examples:

- A patient may say that his wife is his primary caregiver. He wants her to be a part of every medical decision and because he has a hard time remembering things, his wife will be the one to write down information from the doctor. He also gives permission for her to ask medical questions and obtain information on his behalf.
- Another example is a patient whose caregiver works full-time and she attends appointments alone or sometimes will come with relatives or friends. The patient will tell their oncologist or case

manager that their spouse, while unable to attend appointments, is her advocate and she would like him to be informed of every decision by having telephone or email updates from the doctor or nurse or navigator at pivotal times in her cancer care.

- Finally, an adult patient may have his parent attend appointments with him because she is retired and he is unable to drive himself. Her primary job at medical visits is to take notes and be another set of eyes and ears. While this caregiver is there to help her son, the patient may not want his mother privy to medical history or prognosis or asking the doctor questions about cure-alls they discovered online. That information and his boundaries need to be shared with the medical team and his mom!

Not every facility will be flexible enough to accommodate every patient's circumstances but most facilities will be open to having an open line of communication with caregivers and having them be a vital part of the cancer care team.

Here are some tips to remember when interacting with the medical team.

1. <u>You are not the patient</u>. Don't talk to the doctor about your medical history or your illnesses. Remember that you are there for your loved one.
2. Keep notes. Keep a notebook, folder or binder that notates medications, symptoms, side effects and other medical and emotional concerns. Make a copy of the list for the doctor and he/she will be able to assess the patient with some input from you.
3. Encourage the patient to share and be honest about how he/she is feeling. Not all patients will be honest about how they are feeling for fear that their treatments will be stopped or they simply don't want to worry those they love.

DON'T BE AFRAID OF SECOND OPINIONS

There may come a time in the patient's cancer care that they will want a second opinion.

For some patients, the decision to seek a second opinion is a matter of due diligence. They want to confirm that they have made a solid treatment decision by seeing what another set of medical professionals has to say. For other patients, seeking second opinions comes after they believe they did not receive adequate care from their first treatment facility. Some seek second opinions only after they exhaust all treatment options.

Whatever the reason, there can be some stress involved in seeking a second opinion.

MYTH: I want a second opinion, but I don't want to make my doctor mad at me.

FACT: Most doctors welcome second opinions. It tells them that their patient is advocating for their care and that they have the desire to do whatever it takes to get well. Most doctors are confident in their treatment of their patients and know that a second opinion will only confirm what they are already doing. Some doctors have limited resources and will suggest second opinions at larger hospitals or comprehensive cancer centers so that their patients will receive the latest treatment options. Most doctors want the best for their patients, even if it means being treated somewhere else.

If a doctor is ever hesitant in a patient's desire to seek a second opinion-*run*. Getting a second opinion is a patient's right. It is their life they are fighting for.

For most people, a second opinion gives them the confidence they need to move forward with the original doctor's treatment recommendation. For others, it may mean unexplored treatment options.

There are different ways to go about getting a second opinion and as a caregiver, you can help your loved one begin that conversation.

CONVERSATION POINT:

Here are some suggested questions that you and your loved one might use to start a conversation with the doctor about getting a second opinion.

- Before we begin treatment, I'd like to get a second opinion to be sure I'm making the right decision.
- There are a lot of risks to this suggested treatment. I'd like to get a second opinion.
- I've heard a lot about this treatment, I'd like to get a second opinion to see if I am a good candidate.
- I know that you don't have any options for me, but I'd like to get a second opinion.

There may be forms that need to be filled out before medical records will be released. If you have copies of all medical records, you can make copies and provide those to the new facility to save time.

WHAT ARE CLINICAL TRIALS?

[1]The goal of clinical trials is to find out whether new medical approaches that are being developed are safe and effective and better than those currently being used. Most drugs or medical procedures that are available for patients today went through clinical trial testing.

[1]This phase of research is possible only if patients who have the condition that is being studied participate, so a better name for clinical trials would be "patient-assisted research studies." Clinical trials are an important option for people thinking about lung cancer treatments because the newest treatment approaches are being tested in them.

There may come a time in the patient's cancer care that they will explore clinical trials

It's important to know what they are and what they aren't to dispel any myths about them. Clinical trials can be a viable treatment option for people with cancer. There are clinical trials for many different types of cancer.

It's important to know these things about clinical trials.

1. Clinical trials give patients access to the latest drugs, treatments and procedures.
2. If a patient consents to a clinical trial, they can always stop. The choice is theirs.
3. Oftentimes insurance will pay for the clinical trial- but oftentimes the drug manufacturer pays for all costs associated with a clinical trial
4. Clinical trials are not a "last resort". Sometimes there are trials whose goals are to improve current delivery or efficacy of standard treatment. It's important to make clinical trials a part of the conversation at the beginning of the treatment discussion.
5. Patients are not guinea pigs. Patients in clinical trials get quality treatment. They are watched very carefully for side effects and symptoms. Some patients in clinical trials may be monitored more carefully that those who are not.
6. Cancer patients in clinical trials will always receive treatment. They will not receive sugar pills or go without treatment.

CONVERSATION POINT:

Here are some questions you can ask the doctor about clinical trials

- Are there any clinical trials available for my loved one?
- What are the criteria for this clinical trial?
- What are the risks/benefits of this trial?
- Where does this trial take place and for how long?
- Who will be managing my loved one's care in this clinical trial?
- How will we know if it is working?
- What are next steps if it doesn't work?

FINANCIAL ISSUES

Many people facing a cancer diagnosis have financial concerns and issues. There are large issues, like whether or not a patient has insurance coverage and can afford their treatment. Will the patient have to stop working because of their cancer diagnosis and if so, how can they make ends meet? More practical issues like large copays and the cost of prescription medicines, transportation to treatment and medical devices are also top stressors of people fighting a disease like cancer.

Talking about someone else's finances is difficult. Add in a cancer diagnosis and it becomes a really hard conversation. There are things that need to be done and if you are the primary caregiver chances are you will be handling a lot of the financial responsibility while your loved one undergoes treatment.

If you are the spouse of the patient, chances are you know all about your financial obligations and your insurance coverage. If you are the parent, adult child, relative or friend of the patient, your job of deciphering their financial responsibility may be a bit more challenging.

Here are some suggestions to help you get organized and some valuable resources.

1. Take stock of the patient's insurance plan. Understand what the deductibles and co-payments are. Do they provide a case manager?
2. Cancer Legal Resource Center can help direct you to legal assistance and legal resources. (866) THE-CLRC
3. Cancer and Careers can provide information and guidance for those with employment issues. http://www.cancerandcareers.org

4. Social Security Disability is an option for those who are not able to work due to a cancer diagnosis. www.ssa.gov. or 1.800.772.1213

5. Drug assistance programs are available. Drug companies and organizations provide financial assistant to those who cannot afford their treatment medications. https://www.medicare.gov/pharmaceutical-assistance-program/

6. American Cancer Society, Cancer Support Community and Wellness Community may provide assistance with transportation, wigs and other practical needs. Contact your local ACS office.

7. The treatment facility of the patient can also provide a listing of resources that can help with practical and financial issues.

CONVERSATION POINT:

- While you concentrate on treatments, are you comfortable with me helping you with your financial responsibilities? If yes, what exactly do you want my help with?
- In the event you are unable to make financial decisions, will you choose a power of attorney to execute those decisions?

PALLIATIVE CARE- What it IS and what it's *NOT*

What is Palliative Care?

MYTH: Palliative care is hospice care (end-of-life care).

FACT: [2]Palliative care, also known as palliative medicine, is specialized medical care for people living with serious illness. It focuses on providing relief from the symptoms and stress of a serious illness—whatever the diagnosis. The goal is to improve quality of life for both the patient and the family.

Palliative care doctors, nurses and other specialists treat people with serious medical conditions, like cancer. They can help with pain management, symptom management and overall quality of life issues.

Palliative Care includes hospice care when that time arrives **but palliative care also includes pain management, psychosocial support, helping with shortness of breath and management of other side effects. According to the Center to Advance Palliative Care, Palliative care helps with quality of life and can be provided *with* curative treatment.**

It's important to discuss palliative care early in treatment to understand what palliative care services are available at the patient's treatment facility to help your loved one maintain a good quality of life. [2]

Palliative Care is also referred to as "supportive care".

National Cancer Institute definition of Supportive Care (suh-POR-tiv kayr)

[3] Supportive Care is care given to improve the quality of life of patients who have a serious or life-threatening disease. The goal of supportive care is to prevent or treat as early as possible the symptoms of a disease, side effects caused by treatment of a disease, and psychological, social, and spiritual problems related to a disease or its treatment.   Also called comfort care, palliative care, and symptom management. [3]

What are some things that are considered palliative/supportive care?

- Physical Therapy
- Nutritional Therapy
- Respiratory Therapy
- Pain Management
- Chemotherapy – used to manage pain
- Radiation Therapy – used to manage pain
- Emotional- depression, anxiety, fear, family issues

- Financial, legal, employment concerns as well as Advance Directives
- Spiritual

[3]Is there any research that shows palliative care is beneficial?

Yes.

Research shows that palliative care and its many components are beneficial to patient and family health and well-being. Many studies in recent years have shown that patients who have their symptoms controlled and are able to communicate their emotional needs have a better experience with their medical care. Their quality of life and physical symptoms improve.

In addition, the Institute of Medicine 2007 report Cancer Care for the Whole Patient cites many studies that show patients are less able to adhere to their treatment and manage their illness and health when physical and emotional problems are present. To view this report, go to http://www.iom.edu/Reports/2007/Cancer-Care-for-the-Whole-Patient-Meeting-Psychosocial-Health-Needs.aspxExit Disclaimer [3]

[3]Who pays for palliative care?

Palliative care services are usually covered by health insurance. Medicare and Medicaid also pay for palliative care, depending on the situation. If patients do not have health insurance or are unsure about their coverage, they should check with a social worker or their hospital's financial counselor. [3]

CONVERSATION POINT:

Here are some questions you can ask the patient and medical team:

- Does the patient's hospital/treatment facility offer Palliative Care Services?

  _____

- What types of services does that include?

  _____

- Does the patient's oncologist need to provide a referral to begin Palliative Care Services?

  _____

  Does the patient's insurance/Medicare/Medicaid cover the Palliative Care Services offered?

  _____

- Does Palliative Care Services offer support for caregivers and families of patients?

  _____

  What is the difference between Palliative Care Services and Hospice Services at this hospital?

  _____

- Where does the patient receive Palliative Care at?

  _____

[2]Center to Advance Palliative Care https://www.capc.org/about/palliative-care/
[3] National Cancer Institute https://www.cancer.gov/about-cancer/advanced-cancer/care-choices/palliative-care-fact-sheet#q1

ADDITIONAL SUPPORT FOR THE PATIENT

AARP
http://www.aarp.org/
A nonprofit, nonpartisan organization that helps people 50 and older improve the quality of their lives.

AMERICAN CANCER SOCIETY
800-227-2345
www.cancer.org
The American Cancer Society has programs and services to help patients with cancer and their loved ones understand cancer, manage their lives through treatment and recovery, and identify resources for financial assistance.

THE ASSISTANCE FUND
855-845-3663
www.theassistancefund.org
The Assistance Fund is a leading nonprofit organization that provides advanced therapies to the underinsured critically or chronically ill population through a range of services, including education and financial aid.

CANCERCARE
800-813-4673
www.cancercare.org
CancerCare is a national nonprofit organization that provides free professional support services to patients with cancer and their caregivers. CancerCare programs, which include counseling, education, financial and copayment assistance, and practical help, are provided by trained oncology social workers. CancerCare's financial assistance programs provide limited financial assistance for cancer-related costs. The CancerCare Co-Payment Assistance Foundation helps patients afford insurance copayments for chemotherapy and targeted treatments.

CANCER FINANCIAL ASSISTANCE COALITION
www.cancerfac.org
The Cancer Financial Assistance Coalition is a group of national organizations that provide financial help to patients with cancer. The

Cancer Financial Assistance Coalition provides a searchable database of financial resources available to patients in need.

CANCER SUPPORT COMMUNITY
888-793-9355
www.cancersupportcommunity.org
The Cancer Support Community is an international nonprofit organization that is dedicated to providing support, education, and hope to individuals affected by cancer. The Cancer Support Community offers a menu of personalized services and education. These support services are available through a network of professionally led, community-based centers, hospitals, community oncology practices, and online resources.

CANCER AND CAREERS
646-929-8032
www.cancerandcareers.org
Cancer and Careers empowers and educates people with cancer to thrive in their workplace, by providing expert advice, interactive tools and educational events.

CENTER TO ADVANCE PALLIATIVE CARE (CAPC)
Getpalliativecare.org
Provides clear, comprehensive palliative care information for people coping with serious, complex illness. Key components include a Palliative Care Provider Directory of Hospitals, a definition of palliative care, and detailed descriptions of what palliative care does and how to get it. It also provides an interactive questionnaire to assist you in determining whether palliative care might be appropriate for you or a loved one.

GOOD DAYS
972-608-7141
www.mygooddays.org
Good Days, formerly known as the Chronic Disease Fund, provides assistance to underinsured patients who are diagnosed with chronic or life-altering diseases (including cancer) so that they get access to the medications they need.

HEALTHCARE.GOV
Glossary of healthcare terms

HEALTHWELL FOUNDATION

800-675-8416

www.healthwellfoundation.org

The HealthWell Foundation is an independent, nonprofit organization that provides financial assistance to eligible individuals to cover coinsurance, copayments, insurance premiums, and deductibles for certain medications and therapies.

IMERMAN ANGELS

866-463-7626

www.imermanangels.org

Imerman Angels partners anyone, any age, any gender, anywhere and any cancer type seeking support with someone just like them.

LIVESTRONG'S CANCER NAVIGATION SERVICES

www.livestrong.org/we-can-help/navigation-services

Free one-on-one support from The Livestrong Foundation in the areas of insurance challenges, treatment concerns, and more.

LUNGEVITY FOUNDATION

www.lungevity.org

The leading lung cancer nonprofit in the country, LUNGevity is changing outcomes for people with lung cancer through research, education, and support. Lung Cancer HELPLine offers toll-free, personalized support for patients and caregivers at any time along your lung cancer journey. Call 844-360-LUNG (5864)

MY LIFELINE

www.MyLifeLine.org

http://ia.mylifeline.org/getstarted

Sign up for a free MyLifeLine.org patient website, where you can find cancer specific resources, post requests for help or donations and update everyone at once, so you can reduce anxiety and save the energy you need to heal. It's the power of that emotional connection, together with practical day-to-day assistance that can see you through to a more positive outcome.

NEEDYMEDS

800-503-6897

www.needymeds.org

NeedyMeds, a 501(c)(3) nonprofit organization, is an information resource on available patient assistance programs that help individuals who cannot afford medications or other healthcare costs.

PARTNERSHIP FOR PRESCRIPTION ASSISTANCE

888-477-2669

www.pparx.org

The Partnership for Prescription Assistance helps qualifying patients without prescription drug coverage get the medication they need by connecting them to patient assistance programs. This organization offers access to more than 475 public and private programs, including 200 pharmaceutical company programs.

PATIENT ACCESS NETWORK FOUNDATION

866-316-7263

www.panfoundation.org

The Patient Access Network Foundation provides financial support for out-of-pocket costs associated with a wide range of medications to treat a number of chronic or life-threatening conditions, including cancer.

PATIENT ADVOCATE FOUNDATION CO-PAY RELIEF PROGRAM

866-512-3861

www.copays.org

The Patient Advocate Foundation Co-Pay Relief Program provides direct financial support to financially and medically eligible patients, including Medicare Part D beneficiaries. These may include out-of-pocket costs associated with healthcare insurance copayments, coinsurance, and deductibles.

PATIENT POWER

206-232-1542

PatientPower.info

An online information resource dedicated to educating patients living with cancer through video news programs featuring cancer experts and inspiring patients and caregivers, webcasts, transcripts, and live in-person meetings in partnership with leading medical centers, cancer medical societies, and numerous cancer patient advocacy groups.

PATIENT SERVICES, INC

800-366-7741

www.patientservicesinc.org

Patient Services, Inc, is a nonprofit organization dedicated to providing health insurance premium assistance, pharmacy copayment assistance, and copayment waiver assistance for patients with chronic illnesses, including cancer.

RXASSIST

www.rxassist.org

RxAssist, through their online Patient Assistance Program Center, provides a comprehensive database of patient assistance programs offered by pharmaceutical companies as well as other tools and resources to manage their medication costs.

RXHOPE

www.rxhope.com

RxHope is a web-based patient assistance resource that helps patients obtain free or low-cost prescription medications. RxHope has program descriptions and downloadable applications for prescription assistance programs for specific medications.

RX OUTREACH

888-796-1234

800-769-3880

www.rxoutreach.org

Rx Outreach is a nonprofit charity that provides access to affordable medications. Rx Outreach offers more than 600 medications through their mail-order pharmacy to all 50 states, Puerto Rico, and the Virgin Islands.

SAVOR HEALTH

http://savorhealth.com/

Dedicated to making the lives of cancer patients and their caregivers easier and less stressful by providing services that relieve them of the significant time, energy and worry associated with ensuring proper nutrition for themselves and their loved ones.

SURVIVE IT

www.surviveit.org

SURVIVEiT® is the world's first and only nonprofit cancer care rating resource. Developed by survivors for cancer patients, SURVIVEiT® provides anyone affected by cancer with immediate access to the combined knowledge and experience of a global community of survivors, doctors, and allies.

TRIAGE CANCER

424-258-4628

http://triagecancer.org/

Triage Cancer helps survivors, caregivers, health care professionals, and advocates to navigate cancer survivorship though educational events, a national Speakers Bureau, and online tools and resources.

OTHERS:

_____

_____

_____

_____

_____

_____

_____

BECOMING AN

ADVOCATE

DOCTORS VISITS

The first visit with doctors and specialists may feel like a whirlwind and a blur. (Please refer back to *'Learning about the Diagnosis'* for questions to ask the doctor at the beginning of a cancer diagnosis.)

Moving forward, there should be a discussion on what your role as a caregiver is at these doctors' appointments and during treatment visits. If you are not attending doctor's appointments with the patient regularly there are a few things you may want to help the patient consider:

- Does the patient need transportation to/from doctor and treatment visits?
  - You may need to schedule transportation with a car service or with friends and family who can take turns taking the patient to these appointments.
- Does the patient need help talking with the medical team during appointments?
  - Some patients are intimidated by medical professionals and may need the encouragement of an advocate to speak up for them. If this isn't possible, help the patient write down their questions and concerns and have them give that list to the doctor or nurse during the office visit.
- Does the patient need help remembering what is discussed during appointments?

- Sometimes treatments and medications can cause brain "fog" and memory loss. Emotions and medications may make it difficult for a patient to retain and comprehend what is being said during appointments and having another set of ears, notes or a recording device can help.
- What other physical and practical needs does the patient have that may be a barrier to them getting to medical appointments?

_____

_____

_____

_____

_____

Some doctors, nurses and navigators will work with families to follow up via telephone or email. Ask your medical team if this is something they can do on those occasions that someone is not available to physically attend appointments with the patient.

My experience with my dad's medical team wasn't a great one. Keep in mind this was 2002-2003 and "patient centered care" wasn't a common vision at local community hospitals and we had never heard of patient navigators. My dad's oncologist wasn't the most forthcoming when speaking with me or my mom. And many times during those doctors' visits my dad was suffering dehydration, mal-nutrition, extreme nausea, low blood counts, fever and pain. Dad's oncologist wanted to speak directly to him; a commendable but useless effort. Dad was on pain medication and hardly in the position to retain large amounts of information.

I made myself present at every appointment and took copious notes. When the appointment was an important one, I'd bring a tape recorder and record the conversation so that we could replay it later. On those occasions that I could not attend an appointment, we had come to an agreement that the doctors nurse would phone me with an update of the office visit.

When the doctor asked my dad a question I would repeat that question to dad and cause a pause in the flow of the conversation so that dad had time to consider what was being discussed. If it looked like dad was confused or struggling, I would ask the doctor if we could talk about it as a family and get back to him with dad's decision. This worked well at appointments but we still faced challenges during hospital stays.

During hospital stays, one piece of advice I have is to find out exactly when the doctor/specialist will be doing their rounds to the patient and make sure to be there too. Countless times we had left dad sleeping for just an hour or two only to return to find out the doctor had been by to share news of test results or to talk about next steps. The conversation was the same.

"Dad, what did the doctor say?"

"I really have no idea. I think I'll be going home soon."

Nope dad, you have severe dehydration and low blood counts and will be getting fluids and a blood transfusion. How did he misunderstand? Easy to do when you are on oxycodone and confused from being severely

47

dehydrated. If possible, try to always be present during those doctor visits or have the nurse on call phone you with updates.

TALKING TO YOUR EMPLOYER

If you are a caregiver who also has a job outside of the home, you may have concerns about working while caring for someone with cancer. Talk to your employer about what is going on with you. While they don't need to know every detail, let them know that cancer is now a part of your life. The sooner they know, the easier it will be to make advance arrangements, changes and accommodations for your situation and work responsibilities.

If you plan to juggle both a job and caring for someone with cancer, try to set up a support network that will help you because you can't do it all. Set up support for the patient for the times that you can't be available. Set up support at your job for the times you cannot be there. Advance planning and helpful colleagues, friends and family can help during the most difficult times.
If you need to take time off make sure you stay in touch with your employer and colleagues so that things don't fall through the cracks and to let them know that your intent is to come back once things get back to "normal".

Know your rights. Not all employers will be sensitive to your situation.

[4]FMLA

The FMLA provides a means for employees to balance their work and family responsibilities by taking unpaid leave for certain reasons. The Act is intended to promote the stability and economic security of families as well as the nation's interest in preserving the integrity of families.

The FMLA applies to any employer in the private sector who engages in commerce, or in any industry or activity affecting commerce, and who has 50 or more employees each working day during at least 20 calendar weeks in the current or preceding calendar year.

The law also covers all public agencies (state and local governments) and local education agencies (schools, whether public or private). These employers do not need to meet the "50 employee" test. Title II of FMLA covers most federal employees, who are subject to regulations issued by the Office of Personnel Management.

To be eligible for FMLA leave, an individual must meet the following criteria:

- Be employed by a covered employer and work at a worksite within 75 miles of which that employer employs at least 50 people;
- Have worked at least 12 months (which do not have to be consecutive) for the employer; and
- Have worked at least 1,250 hours during the 12 months immediately before the date FMLA leave begins.

49

- An employer need not count employment prior to a break in service of seven years or more unless there was a written agreement between the employer and employee (including a collective bargaining agreement) to rehire the employee, or the break in service was due to fulfillment of military service in the National Guard or Reserves. [4]

There are organizations that can help answer employment issues for those dealing with cancer. One of the organizations I've worked with in the past is Cancer and Careers. This organization has put together a long list of common legal and financial concerns of people impacted by a cancer diagnosis and offers help as you navigate the red tape that comes with a cancer diagnosis. While you can use this resource to help your loved one, you can also find information about FMLA and your legal rights in the workplace as someone who is caring for a family member with cancer.

[4]United States Department of Labor https://www.dol.gov/compliance/guide/fmla.htm

LONG DISTANCE CAREGIVING

Family members and friends who don't live within proximity of the cancer patient, who want to help, are what I call long-distance caregivers. This type of caregiver faces many challenges.

How do you help your loved one when you don't live with them?
Is your loved one being honest about their treatments, their unmet needs and side effects? How can you know for sure? It's a helpless feeling when someone you love has cancer and you are miles away.

Here are some tips to help long distance caregivers.

- Learn all you can about your loved one's cancer and treatment.
- Have a frank conversation with the patient and any primary caregivers about what your role can be. You can offer suggestions of the type of things you are able to help with, but always follow their wishes and cues.

Oftentimes it's the primary caregiver that needs the help the most. You can do things to help them so that they can better help the patient.
If there is a live-in caregiver, there are still ways you can help as a long-distance caregiver:

- Have a conversation with both the patient and primary caregiver(s) and ask them together and again separately how you can help each of them during this time
- Be respectful of the wishes of the patient and primary caregiver
- Give suggestions of specific ways you can help

- Visit when you can to give respite for the primary caregiver
- Research local and national resources and provide that list to the patient
- Continue the relationship you had with your loved ones before they were diagnosed with cancer

While I was the primary caregiver, my mother lived in the home with my father. We had to be aware of what the other was doing at all times. It took several months to get into a grove, but we became a great team working for the best quality of life for my dad.

As the youngest of 6 and only child living near my parents, caregiving naturally fell to me. That didn't stop my other siblings living in different states from trying to help as well. Most of the time they had the best of intentions. One sister insisted we drive half an hour to Whole Foods to get fresh grass-juice every morning for my father to drink. She had read that doing so would cure cancer. We tried it. Dad spit it out. That was the end of that.

Another sibling visited once a month and quoted scripture. He said he wanted to be sure that Dad's soul was saved. Dad didn't seem to mind since he got a visit out of it but I minded quite a bit. I was hyper sensitive about any discussions about death while he was fighting so hard to live. Other siblings came to family outings and just spent time with Dad. He enjoyed the attention and it was a great opportunity to share stories and take photos.

Dad had some great neighbors too. While they didn't help with his physical care, they would periodically mow his lawn or bring over a meal. Some came to visit and chit chat about the weather. The neighbor next door used to come over and raise and lower the American flag he had flying outside our home. Cards of encouragement received in the mail were always a great surprise. Dad really enjoyed having something he could hold, read and display that would make his days a bit brighter.

If there is no live-in caregiver for the patient, organize a team of support for the patient. Delegate jobs to family and friends; for example:

- Be the bridge of information between the patient and their family and friends
    - Share information and updates about the patient via telephone, email, a blog or online group (whatever the patient prefers)
- Arrange for lawn care and/or grocery delivery service
- Arrange for meal delivery or meal "train" of volunteers who can make and deliver meals to the patient a couple of times a week during active treatment
- Enlist neighbors, co-workers and friends to drive the patient to and from appointments
- Make a schedule with these same volunteers to visit with the patient in their home
- Connect with the patient's patient navigator or oncology social worker to tap into local resources

- Visit as often as you can. If you are someone who lives across the country from your loved one, visiting often may not be a possibility, however seeing how things really are in person with the patient can shed light on any unmet needs.
  - Provide respite for the primary caregiver
  - Take the patient on outings and do things that are not cancer-related
- Stay/Get connected with regular phone calls, cards, emails, messages and facetime. Keep the patient engaged as much as he/she is able. Getting calls, cards, and messages lets them know that they are top of mind and cared for

CREATING YOUR CAREGIVER ACTION PLAN (CAP)

The following pages are a general CAP that I created for my patients and their families. Tear it out, or print and fill it out together. This is a document that will house all the information you will need to set the foundation of your caregiving. The intent of a CAP is to encourage communication about important cancer caregiving issues and to set realistic expectations between the patient and his caregiver.

Page one is all about the patient. This is a detailed description of who they are, where they live and the different ways they can be contacted. I encourage patients to be as specific as possible and list their friends and neighbors and any other important contacts that may need to be contacted for any reason.

There is also a section for any accounts and passwords that the patient wants the caregiver to have access to. This could be a social media account, an email account or a financial account that the patient may need help accessing. Contact numbers for the medical team, pharmacy and emergency numbers should also be listed on this page.

While I never lived more than 5 miles from my parents and I visited them every day, there was still so much about them that I did not know. I didn't have the numbers of their best friends. Did they know how sick my dad really was? I didn't know the neighbors across the street. It would have been nice to have them check in on Dad when I was out of town that one week for work. I didn't know where they kept their checking accounts or anything about their healthcare or life insurance. I had to hunt for days for documents. And I did not know what their final wishes were. I took bits and pieces of what I remember them saying when they were alive and I did the best I could. I second guessed myself many times. Had we planned ahead, things would have been much clearer and less stressful.

By implementing a Caregiving Action Plan, you can open the door to those kinds of conversations.

Hindsight and a CAP allows me to ensure that my future caregivers will know what my wishes are and how to best take care of me.

CAREGIVING ACTION PLAN

I.   PERSONAL INFORMATION

Patient's

Name:_____

Street

Address:_____

City, State,

Zip:_____

Phone (home):_____

(cell):_____

Email:_____

Primary and/or Emergency Contact(s)

_____

_____

Nearest Neighbors/Friends

1.

Name:_____Email:_____

Phone:_____

2.Name:_____Email:_____

Phone:_____

3.

Name:_____Email:_____

Phone:_____

Doctors/Specialists Phone Numbers

_____

_____

_____

_____

_____

Nurse's Line

_____

After Hours Hospital Line

_____

Pharmacy Address and Phone Number

_____

Accounts and passwords I should know:

_____

_____

_____

_____

_____

CAREGIVING ACTION PLAN

II.   MEDICATION LIST

MEDICATION LIST

Patient Name: _____ MR#: _____

Date	Medication Name	Strength	Frequency	Physician	Date Discontinued

CARGIVING ACTION PLAN

III.   **TASK LIST**   (to be complete together)

I will help with healthcare tasks as needed such as:

- ☐   Attending medical appointments
- ☐   Asking questions of the medical team
- ☐   Researching treatment options and clinical trials
- ☐   Help with or arrange transportation to and from treatment
- ☐   Administering medications
- ☐   Monitor side effects
- ☐   Assisting with personal hygiene needs
- ☐   Physically assisting the patient when needed
- ☐   Reporting side effects to doctor
- ☐   Manage correspondence

I will help with household tasks as needed:

- ☐   Help or seek outside help for general household chores
- ☐   Help or seek outside help for general lawn care
- ☐   Help or seek help with grocery shopping and meal preparations
- ☐   Pay bills

I will help with legal and financial issues as needed:

- ☐   Help with insurance document and coverage issues
- ☐   Help with seeking financial assistance
- ☐   Help with employment issues
- ☐   Advance directives
- ☐   Living Will / Last Will and Testament
- ☐   Healthcare and Financial Power of Attorney

OTHER:_____

_____

_____

_____

ASKING FOR AND RECEIVING HELP

Asking for help doesn't come naturally for most people. I was raised to be an independent woman. It would make perfect sense that the people who raised me would not easily, or ever, ask anyone for help. I also have a servant's heart in that I always want to help others and as an adult I always wanted to please my parents. They didn't have to ask for my help as a caregiver, I instinctively fell into that role.

There are so many emotions when someone you love is diagnosed with cancer. There may be a heightened sense of mortality, dread and helplessness but you are pulled along by the doctors and medical team and kept busy with learning the logistics of the disease. You are busy with research, treatment options and finding the CT Scan machine and directions to the infusion room. You and your loved one expel your energies into learning how to live and fight cancer.

As the caregiver, you may be rearranging your lifestyle, relationships and responsibilities. I was married with a 4-year-old when my dad was diagnosed with cancer. I was going to school full time and juggling life as a wife and a mom. My life was organized chaos, but it was simple and black and white
Cancer turned everything gray. My dad didn't get the retirement or beach house he had planned for. My mom didn't get that exotic vacation or quality time with dad. He had always worked so hard. He was also so tired. Now he was fighting cancer.

I had to rearrange my schedule to be there to help with doctors' appointments and to administer medications. I anointed myself the meal planner and entertainment director as well. I organized outings and on days he couldn't leave the house we sat together and watched MASH on television. I may not have been able to medically treat or cure my dad's disease but I was going to do everything I could physically do to help him while he was fighting to live. Even when chores had to be done at their house, I helped them do it.

Meanwhile my home was falling apart. I rarely slept. That was the only way I could do homework, spend some time with my family and research treatment options for my dad. I was exhausted. I do not remember a single date or moment of joy unrelated to my dad for an entire year. I have no recollection of my son's first day of kindergarten but I remember the test results from the 3rd PET Scan my dad received. I was the posterchild for caregiver burnout and selfless destruction. I was stress and anxiety and sadness and anger and helplessness rolled into a 5 ft 2 ball of a mess. It's hard to explain to someone on the outside what it feels like to be thrown into stage 4 cancer so suddenly, with no help, zero support and a death sentence for your loved one. I equate it to being kidnapped in the middle of the night out of the comfort of your safe warm bed and thrust into a stark and cold foreign land (medical system)...and sometimes I'd describe it feeling like drowning in a cloudy lake. The emotional weight of everything was SO heavy. It felt like there was no light at the end of that tunnel.

Today, I encourage caregivers to ask for and accept help. I recall numerous times where someone would offer help and my reply was "I'm fine." Or someone would say, "Let me know if there's anything I can do to help." And I didn't take them up on their offer. Looking back, I know that I equated my sacrifices as a sign of how much I loved my parents but it wasn't healthy. I wouldn't let anyone else help. I wanted to do it all myself. In my then-mind, if I did everything myself and I did it right, and prayed hard enough, my dad would survive cancer. Sadly, it doesn't work that way.

I should have said; *I'm tired*. I'm exhausted. I need help with (laundry, lawn, dishes, babysitting, etc.) I could have used a date-night with my husband or a fun outing with my son. I could have asked the many friends who were saying prayers for my dad to help with a chore or a task. I could have organized a meal train or chore list, asked friends to sit with him during his 4-6-hour chemotherapy infusions.

If you are someone who isn't comfortable asking for and receiving help I encourage you to let others in. Don't spend whatever time you have together exhausted and at your wits end. People want to help you. You just have to let them.

Here are some suggestions on asking for and receiving help:

- **Explain your situation.**
  Tell others about what you are going through and how hard it is. *"I am having a hard time taking care of both my parents. When I am here, nothing gets done at home and I feel like I'm neglecting*

my son. Something has got to give. I really need to find some help."

- **Ask for something specific.**

  "Can you pick up my dry cleaning? Would you mind taking dad to treatment on Tuesday? Can you pick Jr. up from school on Friday? Do you mind stopping by the pharmacy? Can you possibly help with the lawn this weekend or know someone who can?"

- **Set up a caregiving calendar for friends and family.**

  Use a printable free template to create a 30-day calendar of caregiving. Add the patient's medical appointment dates to that calendar and then send it to friends and family. Let them know that you are seeking volunteers to help prepare meals, tackle laundry and household chores, transportation to and from treatment, fun visits and outings with the patient to give you some respite. Give many options with the goal of having at least one task on the list that someone else would be comfortable doing.

- **"Let me know if there's anything I can do."**

  Some people say this as a knee jerk reaction to a bad situation. They are putting the ball in your court knowing full well that you won't take them up on their offer to help. Do it. Right then. When someone tells you to let them know if they can help in anyway, say yes! Tell them about your situation and give them specific ways they can help you. They will either step up and help you or they will disappear into the night. Either way you will see who truly wants to help you during your most difficult times.

- **Professional Help**

64

Patient navigators, social workers, counseling, clergy, housekeeping services, home healthcare and visiting nurses are professionals who can help with physical, practical and emotional needs of the patient. Check the patient's medical care insurance coverage and finances to see if it is possible to enlist these types of professionals to help you help the patient.

I remember the many days of cooking meals only to have dad be too sick to eat them. I grew frustrated that he wouldn't or couldn't eat my food. Had I allowed others to help with meal prep I may not have felt that way.

I remember planning treatment days and bringing cold fruit and drinks and puzzle books to keep us occupied. This was a few years before smart phones and mobile internet data plans so it wasn't possible for me to do school work while I was at the hospital. Had I allowed others to sit with him at treatments I could have gotten my work done before 2am, had lunch with my son at school or completed other chores that needed to be done. I could have taken a much-needed nap!

I remember sitting with dad one day watching MASH. It was a show long before my time but it seemed to always be on cable and dad liked to watch it every day. I would look at the TV but I rarely knew what was happening. I would daydream about school work or go over the mental checklist in my mind of what I needed to do when I got home or the next day.

I caught dad staring at me. I smiled at him and he gave me a sad smile back. He told me that I had my own family to take care of and I needed to be there with them. I told him that he was my family and that my own little family understood. I wanted to be there for him as much as I could. We both knew that he may not survive his cancer. And he could see the toll that caregiving was taking on me.

Since then I have heard numerous times from patients that caregivers have the hardest jobs. They take on the brunt of responsibility and get little support. While the medical team supports the patient's wellbeing, the caregiver is left to survive the cancer experience on their own. Most patients want their caregivers to be supported and to seek help.

Remember the flight attendant's instructions to put on your own oxygen mask before assisting others with theirs? Receiving help and talking care of YOU helps you to better take care of the patient!

CAREGIVER FATIGUE

CAREGIVER FATIGUE

It's my opinion that caregiver fatigue happens to everyone at some point during their caregiver role. It's important to recognize signs that lead to fatigue and address them before they lead to burn out. The term "fatigue" seems self-explanatory but it's goes much deeper than lack of sleep or rest. There are many things that lead to caregiver fatigue. Here are a few of those things:

Stress

Many types of stressors can lead to caregiver fatigue. Emotional and financial stress is the most common. Many caregivers are worried about their loved one. Will my loved one survive cancer? How will I handle caregiving and working full time? How will we afford medical care? Can I handle the physical needs of my loved one? Uncertainty fuels stress. Try to focus on the things that you can control for certain blocks of time to shorten the gulf of uncertainty you may be feeling. Surrounding yourself with adequate support can also alleviate many stressors.

Anger

Anger is a strong emotion that impacts almost all the caregivers I've worked with over the years. I know it was something I dealt with in my own caregiving role as well. *Why did this happen to my loved one? Or, how could my loved one let this happen? This isn't fair. Family and friends are not responding the way we need them to respond.*
Anger uses a lot of our energy. Oftentimes there are no great answers to quell our anger. Cancer *isn't* fair. Rather than focus on the things that make us angry, make a list of goals and possible solutions. *My dad's*

doctor isn't aggressive in his treatment or care. Consider adding new members to the medical team or seeking second (or third) opinions until both you and the patient feel secure in the medical team. *My job isn't understanding of my rights or the fact that my spouse has cancer.* Seek help from an advocacy organization that specializes in patient and employment rights. *My family members/friends have disappeared and are unhelpful during this difficult time.* Reach out beyond your existing circle of family and friends for help. Sometimes neighbors, co-workers, church and social groups offer support when those closest to us fall short.

Depression

A cancer diagnosis and major changes in your life-plan can be depressing. Feeling sadness is common for patients and caregivers alike. It is understandable to grieve for the life you once had or the future you once had planned. Sometimes that grief or sadness can be paralyzing, making day to day life unmanageable and/or unbearable. Social workers, nurses, counselors, ministers and chaplains can be helpful resources. These professionals are trained to identify and address depression. Ask for help when you are feeling overwhelmed or helpless.

When I was caregiving for my dad, I combatted feelings of sadness and helplessness by keeping busy. I worked non-stop. I began a nonprofit. I tried to be the best student, employee, wife and mom I could be and I rarely slept. I took the phrase, "one moment at a time" literally. In my case, I didn't fully experience depression until over a year after my dad's diagnosis.

My depression started out as grief and then grew into irritation. I was irritated at my life. I was irritated at the medical community. I became an angry advocate- that person that condemns all other causes except my own- and I became frustrated that people didn't seem to be hearing me. I had lost interest in anything joyful and became very isolated. Positive by nature, I had become pessimistic and moody. My son had been seeing a grief counsellor who struck up a conversation with me one day. I took a chance and began seeing him on a regular basis. Talking to him helped me to develop tools to identify and address my feelings.

I was feeling very alone and lonely. My counsellor suggested that I find a community of support for myself and my family. I found a community church that provided my family with the fellowship and friendship we had been lacking. I have learned that my spirituality is something that is very important to me and I do credit my faith for helping me in my most difficult times.

For some people who experience depression, medication prescribed by their doctor can be a big help. While talking to a professional can help you develop tools to deal with difficult situations, prescribed medication can help with any chemical changes that may be contributing to depression. While you may not get back the life you once had, your present life can be joyful. You can find new hobbies and activities that bring you satisfaction. You may find a new mission or calling from your experiences as a caregiver.
You may also find out that you are stronger than you ever thought you were.

CAREGIVER BURNOUT

According to the Cleveland Clinic, *caregiver burnout is a state of physical, emotional and mental exhaustion that may be accompanied by a change in attitude- from positive to negative and unconcerned. Burnout can occur when caregivers don't get the help they need or they try to do more than they are able- physically or financially. Many caregivers also feel guilty if they spend time on themselves rather than on their ill loved ones. Caregivers who are "burned out" may experience fatigue, stress, anxiety and depression.*

When caregivers don't get the support they need, and are medically and emotionally fatigued, they are at serious risk for caregiver burnout.

Burnout can manifest in many ways. The most obvious signs can be depression, anger, and irritability that doesn't subside. Some caregivers may not recognize the signs of burnout. More subtle signs may be lack of interest or purpose in your life, increased intake of alcohol or stimulants and/or withdrawal from people, groups or activities.

If you think you may be headed for caregiver burnout there are some things you can do to help you cope.

Get physical help.

Enlist help from family and friends. Accept help when it's offered. Hire help when possible. The more physical help you have with caregiving, the less likely you are to experience fatigue and burnout.

Take breaks away from cancer and caregiving.

This is not a luxury- this is a must! You (and the patient) must have what I call "cancer breaks". Spend time with your loved one away from the hospital and treatment. Spend time away from your loved one with friends and family. Do things that you enjoyed doing before cancer. Start a new hobby, see a new movie, or have coffee with a friend.

Taking breaks away from cancer and caregiving helps to bring joy into your life and reminds you of who you were before you became a cancer caregiver and before your loved one became a patient.

Taking care of yourself and getting the support that you need will also help to eliminate resentment that may build against your loved one and a situation you may feel like you have no control over.

Get professional help.

You don't know what you don't know. Professionals can help us identify our physical and mental health needs. Explore different type of medical and mental health professionals that can help you better help your loved one.

RESOURCES FOR

CAREGIVERS

RESOURCES FOR CAREGIVERS

Fifteen years ago, when I became a cancer caregiver, there were no resources for me to tap into. I've researched some organizations that provide emotional and practical support for caregivers and listed them here for you. Not all of them will apply in every situation but it's my hope that you will find one or more resource from this listing that will be of help you.

Organizations that support cancer caregivers:

AARP: https://www.aarp.org/home-family/caregiving/

AMERICAN CANCER SOCIETY: https://www.cancer.org/treatment/caregivers.html

CANCER.NET: https://www.cancer.net/coping-with-cancer/caring-loved-one

CAREGIVER ACTION NETWORK: www.caregiveraction.org/family-caregiver-toolbox

CARING.COM: https://www.caring.com/support-groups/cancer

CDC.GOV: https://www.cdc.gov/cancer/survivorship/caregivers/index.htm

CHI FRANCISCAN HEALTHCARE: https://www.chifranciscan.org/health-care-services/cancer-center/caregiver-resources

DANA-FARBER: http://www.dana-farber.org/for-patients-and-families/caring-for-a-loved-one/

EVERYDAY HEALTH: www.everydayhealth.com/lung-cancer/lung-cancer-caregiving.aspx

HELP FOR CANCER CAREGIVERS:

https://www.helpforcancercaregivers.org/content/respite-care

HENRY FORD HEALTH SYSTEM:

https://www.henryford.com/services/cancer/support/caregivers

LEUKEMIA AND LYMPHOMA SOCIETY:

http://www.lls.org/support/caregiver-support

LIVESTRONG: https://www.livestrong.org/we-can-help/caregiver-support

LUNGEVITY: https://www.lungevity.org/for-patients-caregivers/support-services

 NATIONAL CANCER INSTITUTE: https://www.cancer.gov/about-cancer/coping/caregiver-support

THE CAREGIVER SPACE: thecaregiverspace.org/caregivers-toolbox

THE OHIO STATE UNIVERSITY JAMES CANCER CENTER:

https://cancer.osu.edu/patient-support/support-for-caregivers#!

TODAYS CAREGIVER: https://caregiver.com/topics/cancer/

VERYWELL.COM: verywell.com/caregiving

PSYCHOSOCIAL HELP FOR CAREGIVERS:

FAMILY CAREGIVER ALLIANCE: Offers a family care navigator to help you locate resources: https://www.caregiver.org/state-list-views?field_state_tid=152

WELL SPOUSE ASSOCIATION

A national, non-profit membership organization that provides support to wives, husbands, and partners of the chronically ill and/or disabled through established support groups in communities all over the country.

Caregiver Eligibility:

Any spouse or partner caring for someone who is chronically ill or disabled.

National

(800) 838-0879

Check Support Groups, Contacts list under Find Caregiver Support on website for local offices

http://www.wellspouse.org

CANCER SUPPORT COMMUNITY

Cancer Support Community Helpline: 1-888-793-9355 or to chat live at www.cancersupportcommunity.org

The Cancer Support Community Helpline provides emotional and educational services for all people affected by cancer and their family caregivers.

GRIEF & BEREAVEMENT RESOURCES:

ONLINE GRIEF SUPPORT

http://www.onlinegriefsupport.com/group/losingsomeonetocancer?group
pUrl=losingsomeonetocancer&id=2054931%3AGroup%3A8080&page=2

WIDOWNET.ORG

Online resource that facilitates communication between people about their shared experiences of grief, survival, and recovery after the death of a spouse or life partner.

Online chat, message boards, FAQs

LIFE AFTER

CAREGIVING

LIFE AFTER CAREGIVING

Your loved one will either survive their cancer or they will not. Unless your loved one's condition is chronic, there will come a time when your caregiving stops.

My dad passed away from lung cancer 11 months and 21 days after his diagnosis. While that doesn't seem like a long time, each day was filled with appointments, treatments, side effects and heightened emotions as well as all the other responsibilities that did not cease to exist. It was a very full and very busy 11 months. Just as I had adjusted my life and gotten used to being a caregiver, it ended and life changed again.

For other members of my family, life went on. After the funeral and a respectable mourning period, they picked up their lives and moved forward. It wasn't as easy for me.

I needed to find purpose in my loss and my dad's struggle with lung cancer. I wanted to turn my experience, anger and grief, into something meaningful to benefit others. I needed to share with others what I had learned and I wanted to support other caregivers and patients who were facing what my dad and I faced.

I developed a mission for caregiving and created resources and support for other cancer patients and caregivers because I knew first-hand how isolating and difficult fighting cancer could be. I had a clear career path before becoming a cancer caregiver but when my dad died everything changed for me.

When my dad was diagnosed in 2002, my husband Rick and I created an online support forum called the Lung Cancer Support Community (LCSC). It was a message board for people impacted by lung cancer. It was the first of its kind social network for lung cancer topics and we became a 501 (c)3 nonprofit.

In 2006 I was invited to attend an event called a Livestrong Summit. It was in Austin TX, just 3 hours from my home, so I decided to take a chance and travel alone to this "advocates" event. I had no idea how my life would change or what an advocate was- I just knew I really wanted to do something more.

Some guy named Lance Armstrong was putting on this summit for advocates to change the way people see, treat and live with cancer. It was revolutionary and awe-inspiring. I didn't know anything about him except that he was a cancer survivor. Apparently, he used to be a cyclist too. What I learned from him and his foundation taught me about cancer survivorship and how to advocate for those who couldn't advocate for themselves. Years earlier I had been diagnosed with an early stage cancer. After two surgeries I was considered cured and I tried not to think about it again. Even when I later faced fertility issues I never talked about having had cancer. But Lance called me a "survivor" and I believed him.

I learned about patient navigation and we created personal action plans to address unmet needs. Most of all I learned how I could make a difference and to collaborate with others around the country to make the biggest impact. Some of those Livestrong Leaders are still my closest friends today. So many of us went on to create organizations that have changed the cancer-patient landscape of this country. No matter what you may think about Lance Armstrong as a cyclist, he and his Foundation changed how cancer patients were viewed and treated and set the bar high for other nonprofit organizations. I owe a lot to him and the foundation he created.

Inspired, I went on to create the first-ever lung cancer support group in the state of Texas. This was unheard of outside of the clinical setting but there was a desperate need in my community for lung cancer specific support. Hospital administrators wouldn't work with me to create a lung cancer group because I wasn't a social worker or nurse. I got conference space donated to me through craigslist and advertised this peer-support group across the metro area. At the first meeting, two doctors attended and pleaded with me to move my support group to the hospital so that their patients would be able to attend. Lesson learned here- if there is a will, there is always a way- don't give up.

I didn't know where my future would lead me but I felt in my heart that I was on the right path.

A few of my LCSC message board members created the first-ever lung cancer 5Ks across the country and they wanted to donate 50% of funds raised to my organization. Because I didn't have a medical/science board, I suggested they give the funds raised to LUNGevity Foundation, a lung cancer specific research organization in Chicago, Illinois. LUNGevity's then-president approached me and a collaborative partnership was made.

The LCSC became a service of LUNGevity Foundation and I became a consultant for them.

I also founded the first lung cancer walk in my state as well. I had never even walked a 5K before but I was able to organize one and watch others walk and run it.

Eventually in 2010, I was hired full time to create support and survivorship programs for LUNGevity. I am proud that through the Foundation I created the first of its kinds online support network, peer to peer support program and survivorship programs for people with lung cancer. I think my dad would be proud.

I still take the lessons learned from Livestrong and try to find the unmet needs and underserved patients. That's my mission in life. Helping others helps me make some sense of my loss.

CONVERSATION POINT (*WITH YOURSELF*):

What do you imagine your life will look like when cancer caregiving ends?

Did your experience with cancer change your perspective on life? Have your goals changed?

Can your life go back to the way it was before cancer invaded it?

Can you use your experience to help others?

Over the years patients and caregivers have told me that helping others gives them a sense of purpose and meaning. Others are happy to move past cancer to life as they once knew it.

Life after caregiving can be **anything** you want it to be.

Take some time to reflect on what matters most to you- *then do it.*

Since beginning my cancer advocacy on behalf of my dad, I've met some incredible patients, caregivers and families. My work continues in their honor and memory and I've put into practice these caregiving tips and suggestions.

I've also been diagnosed with a series of autoimmune diseases related to stage 4 genetic liver disease. There is no cure for my progressive disease and it is likely to develop into cancer at some point. Living with chronic illness and pain has given me a personal perspective on what it's like to be a patient- and that makes me a better caregiver.

While I have a great medical team watching my condition and treating my symptoms, there isn't a team of support for my caregiver. Caregiving is absolutely the most difficult job I've ever had. I hope that this guide proves helpful to you.

A CAREGIVER'S BILL OF RIGHTS

I have the right . . .

- To take care of myself. This is not an act of selfishness. It will give me the capacity to take better care of my relative.

- To seek help from others even though my relative may object. I recognize the limits of my own endurance and strength.

- To maintain facets of my own life that do not include the person I care for, just as I would if he or she were healthy. I know that I do everything that I reasonably can for this person, and I have the right to do some things for myself.

- To get angry, be depressed, and express other difficult feelings occasionally.

- To reject any attempt by my relative (either conscious or unconscious) to manipulate me through guilt, anger, or depression.

- To receive consideration, affection, forgiveness, and acceptance for what I do for my loved one for as long as I offer these qualities in return.

- To take pride in what I am accomplishing and to applaud the courage it has sometimes taken to meet the needs of my relative.

- To protect my individuality and my right to make a life for myself that will sustain me in the time when my relative no longer needs my full-time help.

- To expect and demand that as new strides are made in finding resources to aid physically and mentally impaired older persons in our country, similar strides will be made toward aiding and supporting caregivers.

- To _____

   (Add you own statement of rights to this list and then read the list to yourself every day.)

Throughout your role as a caregiver, remind yourself of who you were and who you still are. It's easy to become lost in cancer and daily caregiving. Your mental and physical health is important. YOU are so important in the care and survivorship of your loved one. Remember that.

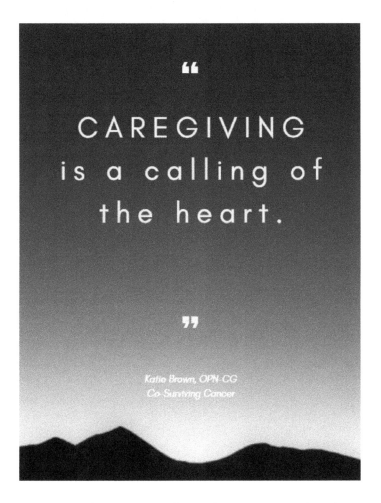

Want to connect with Katie Brown? Visit her at www.iamkatiebrown.com

Navigating Advocacy, a guide to cancer advocacy, is available now.

CPSIA information can be obtained
at www.ICGtesting.com
Printed in the USA
JSHW022143070420
4998JS00010B/1232

9 781979 231688